MARRIAGE:

Will you divorce me if I write a marriage book?
No. I'm never offended. It will be funny.

Illustrated with Crappy Pictures

AMBER DUSICK

ISBN-13: 978-0-373-89307-2

Library of Congress Cataloging-in-Publication Data
Dusick, Amber.
    Marriage : illustrated with crappy pictures / Amber Dusick.
        pages cm
    ISBN 978-0-373-89307-2 (hardback)
1. Marriage--Humor. I. Title.
PN6231.M3D87 2014
818'.602--dc23
                                        2014011071

www.Harlequin.com

Printed in China

To my husband

thank you

CONTENTS

Meet the Crappy Family

We are real people who are really married. All these stories are real and they are really about us.

In these pages you will find some generalizations about men versus women and gender roles and other topics that tend to inspire people to ride high horses or climb on soapboxes or otherwise exert themselves too much. But relax, I'm just talking about us.

Not you, not the rest of the world. I'm sure your marriage is perfect and different and modern. Congrats!

I call my husband Crappy Husband only because I draw crappy pictures. It fit the theme.

It would have been silly to call him Excellent Husband. Plus, that just sounds like bragging.

We also have two kids, Crappy Boy and Crappy Baby. But I'll get to them later.

FIGH
HAPPENS

Although we are joined by marriage, Crappy
Husband and I are still two separate people.
We each have our own opinions, likes, dislikes
and interests. This is highly inconvenient.

CHAPTER 1

TING

A FIGHT A DAY

We fight all the time. Almost every day. However, it is rarely about our relationship, our life choices or our deeply held personal beliefs. It is about something much more important.

Especially when we are going to order in.

Then sometimes after dinner we get to decide which movie to watch.

We don't go to bed angry. But sometimes we do go to bed without having watched a movie.

TEMPERATURE

We haven't yet been able to calibrate our internal thermometers properly.

I always tell him to take off more clothes. He especially appreciates this advice when he is already naked.

Every once in a while he'll let me thaw my hands under his shirt.

But most of the time I have to sneak up on him. He calls it back rape. I call it cuddling.

YOUR OPINION IS WRONG
We mostly agree on music, except when we don't.

It couldn't possibly be that my personal opinion differs from his. It must be that I'm somehow lacking in understanding.

Of course, it goes both ways.

And both of us are huge fans of "You haven't given it a chance!" even when referring to things we've disagreed on for years.

He also occasionally tries out, "You won't admit that I'm right!" but that one just gets laughed at now.

Can't we just agree to disagree? Nah, that's no fun.

HOW I DON'T CUT PINEAPPLES

I don't like to cut pineapples, okay? I just don't. They are big and messy and pokey.

When we have a pineapple that needs to be cut I always bewitch Crappy Husband into doing it. (Notice how *bewitch* sounds so much sexier than *manipulate*.)

First, I feign ignorance and helplessness.

A damsel in distress! Will my brave knight come to slice the pineapple with a few swings of his sword?

Nope, he just offers advice.

So I start to chop up the pineapple by myself. Poorly.

And my knight in shining armor finally arrives! To save the pineapple.

It's not like I'm the only one who uses this method, you know. He really does know how to operate the vacuum, but he somehow convinces me that I'm "just so much better at it" than he is.

HOW HE GETS ME TO DO ALMOST ANYTHING
We have a bunny garden. A bunny garden starts out as a regular garden but then the bunnies hijack it and eat everything.

One day, I decide to build a fence.

I'll just use chicken wire and two-by-fours.

He says "You can't" on purpose. He knows this will guarantee that I'll build a fence. This means he won't have to.

And I fall for it every time.

CREDIT THE SOURCE, OR ARE YOU LISTENING?

I don't like having my content stolen.

We are having a conversation and trying to figure something out.

I suggest a theory, he suggests a theory. And so on . . .

We continue going back and forth for several minutes.

Then he announces:

He says it all proudly. Just look at how smart he is. What he "just thought of" was exactly what I said five minutes ago.

But he will not give me credit and admit that I had just said the same thing.

This is the worst kind of theft. Or maybe he is just not listening.

For example, he does something similar with news.

I tell him something exciting and then several days later:

Yep. Not listening.

PET PEEVES

While Crappy Husband has three pet peeves, I have only one. My pet peeve is that he has three pet peeves. Stupid ones.

First, he thinks I should point the showerhead toward the wall before I get out so that it doesn't spray him in the face when he turns the water on.

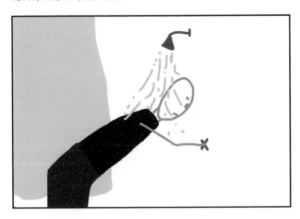

I think *he* should just point the showerhead toward the wall before he turns the water on.

Second, he thinks the small spoons need to be in a separate compartment from the big spoons.

I think that the big and small spoons can get along.

And third, he thinks I should splash water around after brushing my teeth so I don't leave globs of toothpaste in the sink.

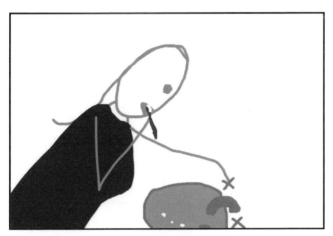

I think he should remember that I'm the one who usually cleans the bathroom. The one who cleans it can dirty it. I'm sure this is written in our household bylaws somewhere.

MARRIAGE IS SHARING

Marriage is all about sharing.

With one exception. Food.

I'm not territorial over food in general. Just ice cream.

He now knows that pints are a single serving.

LISTEN, DON'T FIX

I like to solve problems. I've never been a natural at listening to someone complain while nodding my head in empathy. I'd much prefer to brainstorm ways to fix the damn problem and then move on to eating brownies or something else worth doing. Crappy Husband feels the same way.

However, I admit that sometimes I need to vent and just be listened to.

When this happens, I have to make it very clear to Crappy Husband in order to avoid one of those classic "You're not listening to me!" fights.

Once I'm done, the brownie-eating can commence and everybody will be happy again.

IT'S NEVER HIS FAULT

Crappy Husband doesn't like to admit fault. Even when something is so clearly his fault.

For example, one night he drove to the market to pick up a few things.

The next morning, I discover that the car battery is dead. The interior car light had been left on all night.

Obviously, it wasn't me. I hadn't used the car at all the day before. He was the last one to drive the car when he went to the market after dinner.

I come back inside and say that he left the car light on all night and now the battery is dead. I'm not mad or anything. I'm simply telling him because now we need to jump-start the car.

But he won't admit it! He won't admit making a mistake! Even though we both know that it was him! Instead he just plays dumb and says he doesn't know who it was.

Finally, I say:

Fair enough. It clearly wasn't him. My apologies.

HUSBAND
VERSUS

Before I got married I always scoffed at traditional husband versus wife stereotypes. We'd never be like that. We were modern, intelligent and educated! We were equals! Equal doesn't mean the same. And wow, are we different.

It isn't our fault. Let's blame our ancestors instead. Early men hunted animals and now modern men enjoy stupid shit like sports. Early women were busy searching for berries and now modern women enjoy stupid shit like shopping at Target.

Modern men can't find anything in the refrigerator because their ancestors never lifted up branches to find ripe raspberries. Modern women can't find their way back to their car in a parking structure because their ancestors never wandered through forests looking for wild boar. We can't help it.

CHAPTER 2

WIFE

RUNNING ERRANDS

This is how I pick out dish soap:

I smell them. I look at the ingredients. I compare prices. I contrast the color of the soap with the walls of our kitchen.

And this is how he picks out dish soap:

He texts me to ask what soap he should get.

EMAIL COMMUNICATION

This is an example of one of my emails to him:

> To: Croppy Husband
> RE: Stuff
> July 7, 2014
>
> Well, I feel that perhaps the problem is because last year you said, "XYZ" and I said, "XYZ" too but now it feels like when you said, "XYZ" you really meant, "ZYX" so I think we should talk about...

I can write pages about my feelings regarding our New Year's Eve plans: what I think we should do and why; recalling plans of years past; pros and cons of potential plans, etc.

And this is an example of one of his email replies:

> To: Croppy Wife
> RE: Stuff
> July 7, 2014
>
> Okay.

MAKING NEW FRIENDS

When we go to a party together we have vastly different experiences and goals. He can make friends at parties. I can't.

This is how I make a friend:

It takes years of conversations where we are essentially interviewing each other for the starring role of friend. We also must learn each other's life histories.

And this is how he makes a friend:

He can do this in a matter of minutes. Or seconds, if beer is involved.

VALUING EACH OTHER'S OPINIONS

Sometimes I ask him his opinion on shoes or purses or something.

He always gives the wrong answer.

And sometimes he asks me my opinion on measurements or math or something.

I always give the wrong answer too.

FINDING THINGS

This is how he looks for something:

He stands there and calls for help. If he is really desperate, he might actually tilt his head to view the area from a different angle. But not usually.

And this is how I look for something:

I find it.

SICKNESS

This is how I act when I have a cold:

Normal life only with more tissues.

This is how he acts when he has a cold:

He has the sniffles. The world must stop.

THE LAUNDRY BASKET

This is what I do with dirty clothes:

I put them in the laundry basket.

And this is what he does with dirty clothes:

He throws them near the laundry basket. He says there is a force field around it.

DRIVING

This is what I do to prepare to drive somewhere new:

I map the route on my laptop and phone and then write out the step-by-step directions just in case technology fails.

And this is what he does to prepare to drive somewhere new:

And somehow, he always does.

EATING FOOD

Late at night:

I'm still plenty full from dinner.

This is how he is:

He can't get enough. If he doesn't fill up a cart of food, he'll have to constantly pause the movie to get more snacks.

HOUSEH
RESPON

CHAPTER 3

OLD SIBILITIES

I cleaned the bathroom, did laundry, swept, mopped and put the dishes away.

The dishes that I WASHED.

Both of us suck at this.

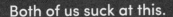

THE WRENCH

Crappy Husband fixed the leaky sink. Yay! I thank him and all that good stuff.

He leaves the wrench on the kitchen counter, so a couple of hours later I ask him where it goes so I can put it away.

He says that he'll deal with it in a bit. Fine.

Two days later the wrench is still there.

Again, I ask him where it goes. Notice I'm not bugging him to put it away. I'm even being courteous and trying to find out where he wants it. But again he says he'll handle it. Fine.

Two weeks later the wrench is still there. I'm quite certain that Crappy Husband cannot see it any longer. It blends into the tile like a chameleon.

So I put it away.

I don't throw it away or do anything evil. I simply put it with his other tools in the garage.

Two seconds later, he points at the counter in pure panic.

He insists that he was just going to put it away.

CLEANING THE HOUSE

We are having friends over, which means we have to clean our house more than usual. Usual being not at all. So we agree to divide and conquer. This is what happens.

Sigh. He was joking. Sort of.

OUR CLEANING WEAKNESSES

The thing is, Crappy Husband and I are equally pretty terrible at household cleaning. To make it worse, we are complete opposites in how we are terrible. He has no follow-through while I can't stop once I start.

He proudly announces that he did the laundry. It's like he expects a medal or a massage or something.

But I know how he does laundry.

He doesn't actually *do* laundry.

He *starts* laundry.

All he does is put clothes into the washing machine and then he walks away. Doing laundry is when you also put the clothes in the dryer, fold the clothes and then put them away.

He is also good at starting the dishes. This is done by filling the sink with hot, soapy water and letting dishes float in it until the water turns cold and the suds disappear.

And he excels at starting to take out the trash. This is done by removing the full bag of trash from the bin, tying a knot in the top and then placing it on the floor next to the bin, without putting in a new bag.

His intentions are there. He just has no follow-through.

Me, on the other hand, once I start something I can't stop.

Cleaning doesn't make anything look clean. It just makes the rest of my house look dirty.

If I upset the delicate balance of general untidiness, then I'll see how really truly filthy my entire house is, and the angry cleaning beast will wake up. The angry cleaning beast will go on a swearing/cleaning rampage that lasts for several days until she finally collapses while wiping down bottles of cleaning products and bars of soap with a damp washcloth.

I'm powerless against the beast once the metamorphosis happens. So it's better to avoid cleaning as much as possible. Especially since it looks the same two days later either way.

THE COCKROACH BATTLE
I go into the bathroom to brush my teeth before bed.

I'm startled by a large brown cockroach climbing up our shower curtain.

Crappy Husband runs into the bathroom saying, "What is it?!"

I expect him to walk over and pick it up with his hands and take it outside as he usually does with living crawlies. Bug removal is in his husband job description. But he just stands there staring at the cockroach.

He backs out of the bathroom with his hands in the air as if he's surrendering. His eyes are wide and fixed on the cockroach.

You know how most people have random irrational fears? I have several. So far, he has only one. Cockroaches.

We stand in the hallway and try to assign the job of cockroach soldier.

I tell him to be brave, that I'll be right there behind him in battle.

He tells me that the cockroach always wins, so battle is suicide. Finally, we agree to do it together.

I go to the kitchen to grab a broom while he rifles through closets. We meet back in the hallway. He looks ridiculous.

He has on a knit hat, goggles and bright yellow kitchen gloves. He explains that his biggest fear is the cockroach touching his head. Or his skin.

Our plan is that I'll hit the cockroach with the broom and once it is dead, he'll pick it up and flush it down the toilet.

We take a deep breath and enter the bathroom.

Boldly, I walk right up to the shower curtain, holding my broom like a baseball bat. Crappy Husband is standing behind me.

I swing as hard as I can.

But at the last moment, the cockroach moves and instead I just hit the curtain, sending the cockroach careening through the air over my head.

And right toward Crappy Husband's head. He drops to one knee and tries to shield himself as he prepares to die.

But it just misses him and lands on the floor.

It scurries toward my bare feet. I scream, throw the broom to Crappy Husband and try to jump up onto the toilet. The lid of the toilet isn't down, so my feet perch on the slimy rim.

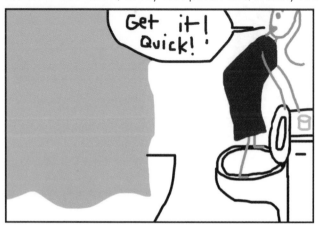

I almost slip and I scream at him to get it. He realizes he has survived the attack so he picks up the broom and smacks it down on the cockroach. He gets it.

However, he slams it down so forcefully that the broom snaps in half.

He's still afraid of cockroaches.

COOKING
Crappy Husband cooks. I cook sometimes too.
This is how he cooks:

He measures things and will not deviate from the recipe. If a recipe calls for seven celery sticks and we only have six, he will panic and go to the market. I'm not exaggerating.

If a recipe calls for 10 ounces of tomato paste and we have a can that is 12 ounces, he will measure it out and not use the measly extra two ounces. Must. Follow. Recipe.

He also uses every single pan and dish in the entire kitchen. I have no idea how a recipe with only three ingredients requires nine bowls, but it usually does. I'm very, very grateful for his cooking, but I loathe the food explosion in the kitchen after he is done.

This is how I cook:

Recipe amounts and ingredients are just *suggestions*. I approach cooking like an abstract painting. It's art.

I clean as I go. I'm often washing the dishes and not noticing that things are burning or that my soup is boiling over. But at least the kitchen gets cleaned up.

Guess who's the better cook? Hint: It isn't me.

CARS IN THE COUCH

Once kids enter the picture, more stuff enters the picture. And less time to clean up all the stuff. As much as we could blame them, it really is our own doing.

Crappy Husband is looking for the remote so he lifts up one of the couch cushions.

He is shocked by what he sees, so I explain:

The kids pulled up the cushion and played with cars there once.

Yes, I did. About three months ago.

And with that he simply replaces the cushion on top of the cars, sits down and says, "Guess not."

THE CAT LITTER

We have two Crappy Cats. For years and years I was the one who changed and cleaned the litter box. Then I got pregnant and Crappy Husband took over because that's the way it works if you read a pregnancy book and get paranoid. Not that I complained about relinquishing my duties.

Now, several years later:

He really can't argue with this.

JUST BLOOD

Crappy Husband walks into the bathroom and sees a huge brown streak splattered across the white fabric shower curtain.

I reassure him that it isn't poop. Just blood.

He shrugs and walks away.

This story sums up the state of cleanliness of our house. A pint of blood smeared in the bathroom? No big deal. At least it isn't poop.

(It was hair dye, by the way.)

INTERESTS
ENTERT

&
AINMENT

This is the stuff we do now that we are old and boring.

WAY TO A MAN'S HEART

The way to a man's heart is not just through food or his penis.
There is another way.

Obscure *Star Wars* references.

CLASSIFIED AD

Of course, sometimes our interests don't match up. I could live in a
fabric store while he starts to die upon entering one. He could talk
about guitar amps for ten hours while I can only pretend to listen
for ten minutes.

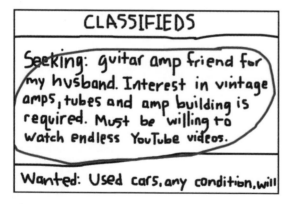

This is my official classified ad. Email guitarampfriend@gmail.com
if interested. I can pay in beer or wine.

HOBBIES

We both have tons of hobbies. This makes life fun. And cluttered.

I can't get rid of anything that might possibly be used or repurposed in the name of arts and crafts.

And I can't help but collect things that might possibly be used or repurposed in the name of arts and crafts.

Crappy Husband tries to talk me out of it, saying it isn't a chair, it's just junk. But I know better. Someday I'll refinish it and reupholster it and it will be a lovely chair. Someday. For now, just stick it in the garage with the others.

It pains me to leave things with potential behind. They need me! Or what if two months from now one of our chairs breaks and we need a replacement? I should take this one as backup!

But he is just as bad. Worse, really. He won't get rid of anything.

So of course we have to keep it.

EXCHANGING GIFTS

When we were dating, we'd surprise each other with gifts for birthdays and holidays. A lot of time and energy went into selecting the perfect item.

We're married with kids now. We don't have time or energy.

So now we both just tell each other what we want. Sometimes we'll just go ahead and buy it for ourselves and then say, "Hey, thanks for the birthday shoes you bought me today! I love them, they're perfect!"

The types of gifts have changed too. There is always an extreme lack of handcuffs, sex dice and edible underwear under our Christmas tree.

We exchanged a tea kettle and a cozy blanket. Because that is what we wanted. We just want to be comfortable and cozy. Like elderly people. And you know what? It's great. Edible underwear tastes horrible anyway.

HAPPY ANNIVERSARY & TUBBIN'

We're sitting on the back patio and the kids are asleep. It's our anniversary. We start talking about how nice it would be to have a hot tub.

We've wanted a hot tub for a long time. A hot tub is like a bath you can take with your friends. A hot tub has just the right amount of sharks. It's healthy and lowers stress, just like joining a gym, but it is cheaper in the long run. Plus, we're more likely to stick with it!

But we don't have one. And it isn't going to magically appear for us.

Sigh. I look out over the yard. I notice the blue plastic kiddie pool. It's just sitting there looking lonely.

I jump up and drag it over onto the cement of the patio.

I have a plan and I will not stop until I have a hot tub. First, we fill every pot in our house with water and start heating them on the stove. Then we fill bucket after bucket after bucket of hot water from the kitchen and garage and lug them out and pour them into the pool.

It is exhausting.

Finally, we are done! We grab a bottle of wine, take off some clothes and get in our DIY tub.

It is pure bliss. Just. Perfect. Sure, I can only get half of my body underwater at any one time, but half relaxed is better than not relaxed at all.

All that work carrying buckets was so totally worth it! We should do this every night!

Crappy Husband isn't so sure.

But I can't do this alone the next time. He has to be on board!

So I offer the only thing I can think of. (No, not a blow job. Come on, it isn't like there's ice cream on the line here. Just a hot tub.)

A massage. I even offer to get the coconut oil! I love coconut oil, and it will be good for our skin!

I finish my glass of wine, hop out of the tub and go inside to grab the coconut oil. When I settle back in the tub I scoop out a large dollop with my fingers. It smells heavenly. Just what we need to take this tub up a notch on the relaxation scale. It is like we are on a tropical vacation. I drink some more wine.

After the massage, I drink some more wine. Then I get more coconut oil and spread some on my arms like a lotion. There are now swirls of oil on the surface of the water. We're stewing in a drunken hot coconut bath.

Wow, it's really oily in here!

It is getting really drunk in here. I think we should get out.

I start to stand up and my foot slips on the slick, coconut oil–lubricated bottom of the pool. I fall back and splash down into the pool.

It isn't so funny when he falls too. To make matters worse, the cement around the tub is wet and slick with oil from my splash. It is too slippery to get out of the tub! We could fall on the cement and crack our heads open like coconuts.

What will we do?

Obviously, the safest thing to do is to wait out here all night long. The kids will wake up in the morning and come looking for us and they'll call 911 or the fire department or the Frog brothers or whomever one calls when your parents are stuck in a hot tub.

But sometimes the safest choice isn't the right choice. We're gonna have to risk it.

Crappy Husband realizes he can reach one of the lounge chair cushions, so he pulls it off and lays it down on the cement toward the back door. A cushion bridge.

We just have to slither out of the pool like snakes onto the cushion.
We can't stand up, we can only glide.

But it works! And we get inside safely. Best anniversary ever.
Who needs a hot tub?

EXTREME DIYNESS

We suffer from a condition called DIYness. If you are unfamiliar with the term, it stands for do-it-yourself-ness. We love DIY. But we love it beyond our abilities.

It usually starts the same way. We want something. It costs money.

We'll DIY!

We look up tutorials and plans. We research wood. We research stains. Types of lids, hinges and locks. We figure out dimensions. We become obsessed with our project. We'll save so much money! We're so frugal!

Finally, we head to the lumberyard and buy wood. And wood glue. And various grits of sandpaper. And wood pegs. And new blades for our saw. And stain.

At this point, we pay no attention to how much all of this costs but it is roughly much more than a hundred bucks. It doesn't matter. Once the DIY symptoms begin, we are no longer rational. It's a disease.

We measure and we build and we sand and we stain and we sand again and we stay up way too late and we get sweaty and we work our asses off and then finally:

No, we didn't save money. No, we didn't make a nicer toy box. But it is still better. It is personal and made with love. (DIYness will always prevail. Hey, I'm not interested in a cure.)

SPORTS

While we share a lot of interests, we also share a lack of interest in one thing. Sports. I don't follow sports and neither does Crappy Husband. I'm so thankful.

My entire extended family, on the other hand, does follow sports. Intensely. They live in Wisconsin so they are Packers fans. That is a football team. Some of my family members wear certain clothes during games because they believe it brings the team luck. They eat or drink certain things when a touchdown is scored and game nights require grilling marathons and celebrations and drinking and friends. Actually, minus the sports part, it is all really fun.

When we visit, we try to fit in as best we can and everyone is very accommodating of our complete and utter lack of sports knowledge. (*Although I did once get blamed for the Packers losing Super Bowl XXXII because I didn't cheer with enough enthusiasm. So sorry about that, Wisconsin.*) We are clueless. We don't even know the names of the characters. I mean players. See?

One year at Thanksgiving we all went around saying what we were thankful for and what we hoped for in the coming year.

Crappy Husband stood up and said a bunch of lovely things he was thankful for and things he hoped for. To loop in my family, he decided to make a sports wish for them:

He will never hear the end of this.

WE CANNOT ATTEND

Sometimes we get invited to something and we aren't going to go. And we have a very good reason for not going. We don't *want* to go.

Unfortunately, being polite trumps honesty in our culture, so we have to come up with a "real" reason for not going. Crappy Husband can't lie, so turning down invitations is always my domain. I don't like to lie either, but, fortunately, I've come up with a workaround.

I tell Crappy Husband what I said.

He is appalled that I lied. But, you see, I didn't lie!

It's all in how you say it. "Unfortunately, we can't attend. We're going to a birthday party for a friend." Both of those statements are true, they just aren't related. It's true, we really are going to a birthday party. And it's true, we really can't attend.

It isn't my fault if the person connects the two statements together.

MO

The problem with money is that it is super-fun to get rid of it.

WHERE THE MONEY GOES

Where does it go? I could blame the kids and how they eat a single bite of a banana and then say they are done. I could blame our assorted DIY projects and hobbies. I could blame the fact that we live in an expensive area of the country. I could blame a lot of things, but this is the real truth. This is where the money goes:

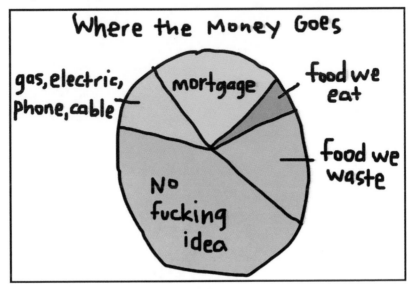

SPENDERS VERSUS SAVERS

Apparently, some people are spenders and some people are savers. Classic couple trouble happens when you have one of each in a marriage. One person consumes expensive designer clothes or electric tools, while the other person saves twist ties from bread bags and reuses coffee filters.

When we first got married, we didn't have this problem. We had a different problem. We were *both* spenders.

Hey, did anyone pay the electric bill this month? We've never forgotten long enough for our lights to be shut off. But we've certainly enjoyed our share of late fees for this sort of thing.

Two kids and a mortgage later, we've had to become a little bit smarter about this so the lights don't actually go out, but we're still not as responsible about money as we should be. We're still not savers. We're at an in-between level that I call save-to-spenders.

We don't save to save. Now we save to spend. We still have a lot to learn. But at least we pay the electric bill first.

THE CABIN IN THE MIDDLE OF NOWHERE

I grew up in a rural area of the Midwest. Things were cheaper there. When we start to worry about money, I stress about the expensive area that we live in. You can't even buy romaine lettuce for less than a dollar here! We're gonna starve!

Which results in panic:

"I'm serious!"

"We can't grow our own food in the garden we already have; we're terrible gardeners!"

"Yeah, but I don't mind hard work and we'd be better at it if we were in the middle of the woods."

"Why?"

"But it would be so much cheaper!"

"There is a good reason it is cheaper!"

"Why?"

"Because nobody wants to live there."

"Hey, can you run to the market? We're out of romaine lettuce."

"Sure, as long as we don't have to move to a cabin in the middle of nowhere."

"Fine. It's a deal. We won't move. At least not this month."

SOMEBODY STOP US

If I were pining over diamonds and he were pining over platinum golf clubs, we could argue each other out of buying these over-the-top things. Well, the good news is that I don't wear much jewelry and he doesn't play golf. The bad news is that the things I want to splurge on are the things he also wants to splurge on.

This means there is nobody here to stop us.

But at least we can drown our regret with good wine.

THE CAREER SWITCH DEBATE

When we start stressing about money, sometimes we decide that maybe we should drastically change our careers. Big results require big change, right? Plus, when you're having money worries, the responsible thing to do is to take out a giant business loan for a vocation you have zero experience in.

We've recognized this pattern, so now our conversation is always the same:

See, that's the thing. We often think we want something, but we're wrong. What we really want is much simpler.

Take opening a restaurant. Sure, we want to open a restaurant. Doesn't everyone? The food! The atmosphere! But wait. Do we really want to spend every night there and manage staff and deal with customers and basically live there? No. We just want to go out to eat at a restaurant.

Or running a bed-and-breakfast! Everyone thinks they want to open a bed-and-breakfast. Me too! Such a romantic idea! Oh, how lovely and relaxing it would be! But it is all a facade. I don't want to wash sheets and serve people and deal with reservations and angry travelers. All I really want is to *go* to a bed-and-breakfast and read novels on a bench in the bucolic countryside with lavender in the air.

This conversation ends with us realizing that what we really want is to just go to a club, restaurant and a bed-and-breakfast. Simple right? Except all of those things cost money. Darn.

WHO SHOULD MANAGE THE MONEY

Marriage and financial experts say that the person who is best at managing money should be the one in control of balancing the finances. We can't follow this advice. It would look like this:

Mama, you have $11 to buy groceries. Papa, no more tacos for lunch.

At least potentially. He's only six. We're grooming him for this position. He'll let us know how much we can afford to pay him to be our accountant later on.

BALANCING THE BUDGET

Everyone knows that money stress is the source of many divorces. So we decided to take a class in financial planning to try to get better at this stuff to, you know, avoid divorce. One of the rules of the class is that we must sit down together and make a monthly budget at the start of each month. Everyone warned us that this is something known to cause huge fights among couples.

We have to write down how much income is coming in that month and then deduct every single expense for things like gas and electricity and the phone. The regularly occurring bills. And anything left over has to be accounted for too. Every dollar has to have a name on it, even if it is just going toward debt or savings or birthday gifts.

Apparently, most people do this regularly or at least have done it at some point. This was our first time. It hurt at first but we got the hang of it. It only took us three hours.

What was everyone whining about? We totally rocked this. We didn't even fight.

We explored the idea of not eating for a month, but ultimately decided to start all over.

And then the huge fight began, trying to come up with a way to lower our monthly grocery budget.

It was classic and ridiculous. But eventually, we moved beyond blaming and anger and started to make fun of ourselves.

Laughing got us through and we managed to figure it out. Still thinking about the grocery store and toilet paper ideas though.

HEALTH
HYGI

Farting and pooping
and not showering.
Being married is delicious.

CHAPTER 6

&

ENE

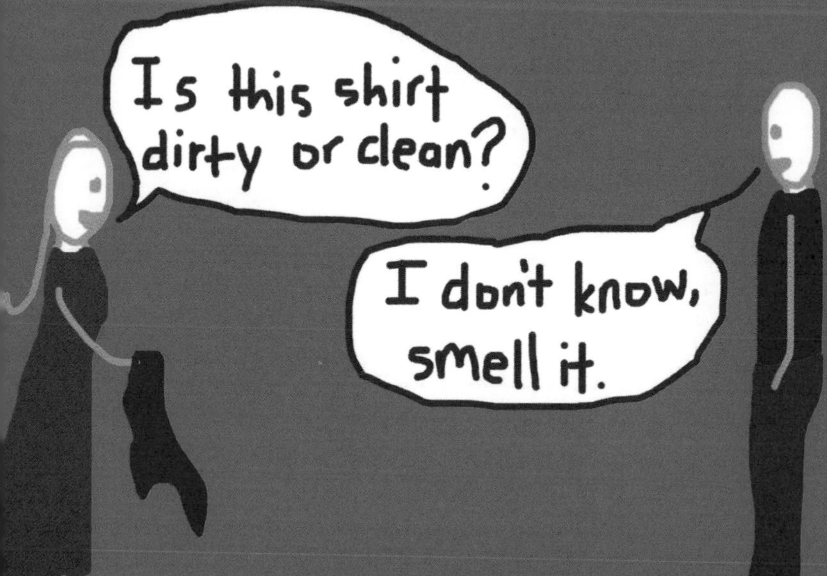

FARTING IN FRONT OF EACH OTHER
Guess what? Everybody farts.

Some people wouldn't dream of farting in front of their spouse. That's cool. Whatever works. But for us, we would have been divorced by now if we weren't allowed to fart in front of each other.

I can't imagine! How uncomfortable would it be to not feel fart-safe in my own home?! I'd have to get up while watching a movie to go fart in another location. Over a lifetime, that is a whole lot of farting in secret. I'm getting tired just thinking about it.

Now this is love.

A LINE HAS BEEN DRAWN

We fart in front of each other. We also pee in front of each other. But even for us, we have to draw the line somewhere. The line is at poop. Sure, we can openly admit that we poop, like that time at a deli recently:

But doing it in front of each other is strictly off-limits. Who would want to do that anyway? Don't answer that. And definitely don't look it up online.

I've also added one additional pooping etiquette rule:

He cannot talk to me through the door. He always tries to, seeing as he has me cornered and all, but I won't engage. Those two minutes where I lock the door and ignore the kids banging on it are sometimes the only two minutes alone I get all day. Everybody, go away!

SHOWERING (OR NOT)

I love the smell of Crappy Husband's sweat, but I don't know anyone who likes the smell of overripe feet.

Really, it was more of a request than a question.

EXERCISE AND LOSING WEIGHT
You know what it takes for me to lose weight?

Exhausting exercise every day and a diet of kale and water.*

After two weeks:

I don't really eat only kale and water. That would be stupid and unhealthy. Though probably fairly effective.

This is what it takes for Crappy Husband to lose weight:

He thinks about losing weight so he'll throw in a push-up or two between gorging himself on high-calorie, delicious foods.

After two weeks:

DIRTY CLOTHES

After I wear an article of clothing, it goes in the laundry basket to be washed.

After Crappy Husband wears an article of clothing, it doesn't go into the laundry basket. It goes anywhere but the laundry basket.

When Crappy Husband comes home, he randomly takes off his clothes while walking through the house. This means his pants will wind up in the dining room, his socks on the kitchen counter and his shirt on the couch.

Why? Why?

His measure for whether clothing is dirty is totally different than mine too. To me, if something has been worn it is dirty. But to him:

Only when it reeks is it laundry basket–worthy. As I mentioned in Chapter 2, even then it doesn't go *in* the laundry basket. Just *next* to it.

THE SUITCASE

When Crappy Husband returns home from a trip, he puts his suitcase next to his dresser. A day goes by. Another day goes by. More days go by. More. The suitcase just sits there. Annoying me.

For two weeks.

I refuse to clean it out for him. This is totally not my job. I'm not going to touch it. The suitcase eventually gets hidden in the corner of our room.

Several months later he has to go on another trip and gets his suitcase, which is still full. His last trip was months ago!

UNDER WHERE? UNDERWEAR

If you want to know if a couple is married or not, just look at their underwear.

When we were dating, I wore matching bra and underwear sets every time we were together. I acquired quite a collection. And a large credit card debt to prove it.

Now I have one pair of "good underwear" and one decent bra for special occasions only. And they don't match.

He, on the other hand, still has tons of pairs of underwear. They are the same ones he was wearing the year we met.

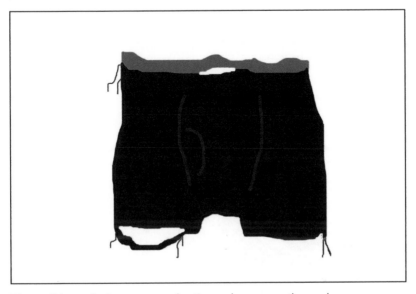

They all have holes, saggy elastic and are see-through now. But hey, that just makes them sexier.

GROWING OLD TOGETHER

When I was single, I wanted to "find someone to grow old with" and I had visions of sitting on a porch swing together with gray hair sipping lemonade.

That was a terrible goal. If I were smart when I was young, my goal would have been to "find someone to stay young with" because getting old isn't actually very much fun. And we don't even have a porch swing.

We do, however, sit on our patio and sip wine (it's like lemonade) and this is what it is really like to get old together:

We can also have entire conversations determining who is more tired.

(Apologies to the person who is older than I am and is now all bent out of shape after reading this. Sort of like how I get annoyed when I hear people in their twenties sweating turning thirty because they'll be SO OLD. I know. It's all relative. How old am I right now? Well, I'm the oldest I've ever been. So really, how could I know any better?)

APPENDICITIS

I'm eight months' pregnant. I've also fractured my metatarsal, which means I have to wear a huge plastic boot on my left foot. This adds a limp to my waddle.

One night we go out to eat at a new Chinese restaurant and afterwards Crappy Husband says his stomach feels weird. We blame the food. But it continues to feel weird and in the wee hours of the night Crappy Husband determines that he might have appendicitis.

I drive him to the hospital. When we arrive in the emergency room, we're yelled at by various staff members and well-meaning passersby that we're in the wrong place. Labor and delivery is somewhere else.

After finally getting the message across that we are not here for me, Crappy Husband is seen by a doctor. It turns out he does indeed have appendicitis and his appendix needs to come out immediately.

Surgery goes well and he has to spend the following night there to recover. I decide that I want to stay over too.

Early in the afternoon, I ask for a cot. No cot comes. I ask again. None. I ask again. And again. All the nurses keep telling me that one is coming. It is just that they are very busy and all the cots are being used. I'm not angry. I'm just tired. And uncomfortable.

At midnight, I give up and fall asleep on the cement floor on an extra sheet from the closet.

At about 3:00 a.m. a nurse comes in to check Crappy Husband's vitals and finds me there:

But even she can't source a cot. She finally steals a few sofa cushions from the staff lounge for me to lie on. They smell like ass but feel like heaven.

The next day, Crappy Husband is discharged and starving, so we head to the market to get some groceries. He is very sore, so I urge him to stay in the car but he wants to come in. Looking at him, you'd never know he just had surgery.

I buy several bags' worth of food and start to carry them out. He can't lift anything, of course, and certainly not heavy bags.

Just then we realize how ridiculous this must seem to others.

He looks like such a lazy jerk, making his hugely pregnant and injured wife carry everything! I fought the urge to announce to everyone that he had just had surgery.

I took pride in the fact that, despite being hugely pregnant and having a fractured foot, I was the stronger one between us at that moment. Of course, a month later, he had healed and our son was born, and then he carried the groceries.

PAREN

CHAPTER 7

TING

Nothing shakes up* a marriage like a baby.

*I don't mean *shakes up* like what you do with a martini shaker, resulting in a delicious beverage. It's worse. It's more like building a roller coaster over your house that constantly rumbles and shakes all of your belongings onto the floor and then you have to glue the pieces back together. Messy, but worth it.

NAMING THE BABY PROBLEMS

One of the coolest things about having a child is that you get to name the child! All by yourself! Anything goes!

Unless you are married to or partnered with or otherwise on speaking terms with the other party responsible. Then, unfortunately, it is customary to allow them to have an opinion. Sigh.

And opinions he had. He nixed every name I suggested for one stupid reason or another.

Suggesting names became like a word association game. He always knew someone or it reminded him of a movie or a song or a street he once skinned his knee on when he was seven. Every name had something bad connected to it.

And sometimes his veto was just in the form of a rhyme.

Frustrated, I'd ask him to make some suggestions:

He was usually super-helpful.

WHO WILL THE BABY LOOK LIKE?

We spent hours daydreaming about what our first child would look like.

Will he have curly, light brown hair? Or straight black hair? We looked at baby photos of the two of us and tried to imagine.

When Crappy Boy was born, days of grueling labor and complications ended in a cesarean section. They quickly whisked him away to a warmer table.

Does he look more like me? Does he look more like Crappy Husband? I didn't get to see!

He then went on to say that he looked like his brother and his great-grandfather too. Finally, a nurse pointed out that the baby in fact looked like *him*. Imagine!

(Now I'm told that both my kids look like a balance of both of us, but I know people are just being nice. I was merely a vessel for his genetic material. All of mine got tossed.)

TAKING CARE OF CRAPPY BABY

This is how I take care of Crappy Baby:

And I still get a ton of other stuff done.

This is how he manages to take care of Crappy Baby:

Was this because he was so completely enraptured that all his focus and attention were on the baby? Sometimes. Maybe. Nah. Babies are like paperweights for men. He's not enraptured: He just can't move. The presence of a baby in his arms makes him incapable of doing anything else.

WHAT I THINK HIS DAY IS LIKE AND WHAT HE THINKS MY DAY IS LIKE

Sometimes I get jealous when he goes to work. With other adults. He gets to have stimulating conversations!

It is probably like this:

And of course sometimes he gets jealous of me staying at home, "relaxing." He thinks it is probably like this:

Really, we're both off.

This is what it is really like for him at work:

And this is what it is really like for me at home:

But at least we have something to talk about when he gets home.

FREQUENTLY ASKED QUESTIONS
Kids ask a lot of questions. I would guess the most common one they ask is something like this:

But the most frequently asked question to Crappy Husband has got to be:

Mostly because I often say yes to the cookie one.

HOW BABIES ARE MADE

I'm all dressed up to go out on a date night with Crappy Husband. We're about to leave and drop the kids off at their grandparents' house.

Apparently, I don't get dressed up very often.

WE'RE SO UNCOOL
Nothing turns you into an old person quicker than having a child.

The whole family is in the dining room, looking at the new anatomy set that Crappy Boy got as a gift. He points to the bones between the hand and the elbow and asks why there are two bones there instead of just one.

Crappy Husband explains a little bit about the radius and the ulna and then gives Crappy Boy the thumbs-up sign and says:

But Crappy Boy just looks confused.

Finally, he says:

So I explain that it means "cool" or "awesome," but that people don't use it as much anymore.

Then Crappy Boy says:

And he goes on to say that Pops, his grandpa, says *nifty* sometimes.

Rad.

BEDTIME ROUTINE

We take turns doing the bedtime routine with the kids,
but Crappy Husband isn't very good at it.

The only person he can get to sleep is himself.

MY PARENTING VACATIONS

It is the end of a very long day. The kids have fought nonstop.
The house is a disaster. I need a vacation.

Don't worry. I always return from vacation early.

PARENTING METHODS

Crappy Husband doesn't read parenting advice books, he doesn't read parenting advice blogs and he certainly doesn't care about the various "parenting styles" that parents label themselves with. He thinks it's mostly a waste of time.

I, on the other hand, devour everything, especially when we're dealing with a new, challenging behavior by one of the kids. Since Crappy Husband doesn't read the books, I give him a brief synopsis of each one and it always goes something like this:

I tell him all the things we've been doing wrong and what we should be doing instead.

Then he reminds me that last week it was something different and that next week I'll be saying something totally new. It's like I'm in my very own Parenting Book of the Week book club. By the time I narrow down how I truly think we should start dealing with the behavior, it stops.

OUR WEDDING ANNIVERSARY

I remember our last pre-kids wedding anniversary. I was pregnant with Crappy Boy.

We went to a fancy restaurant, just the two of us. We daydreamed about how great it was going to be to have a family.

More than a handful of years and two kids later, we recently celebrated another anniversary. This time at home. With the kids.

Here's to having a family!

We were right though. Having a family *is* pretty great. Just rarely during dinner.

SEX & ROM

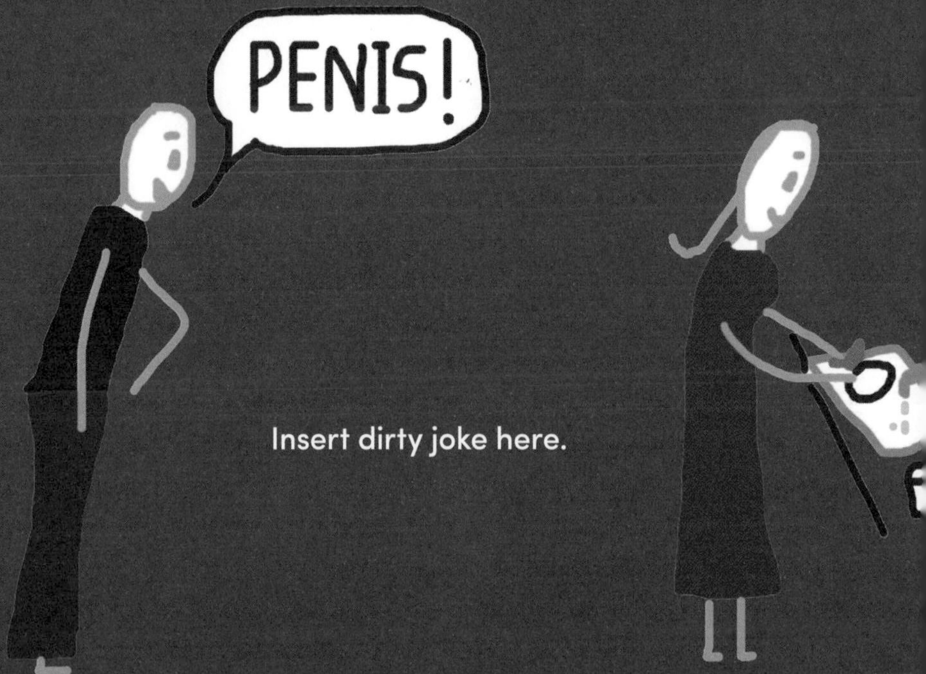

Insert dirty joke here.

CHAPTER 8

ANCE

HOW TO MAINTAIN A HEALTHY SEX LIFE

We have different thoughts on how to keep our sex life robust.

I'd like this to happen occasionally:

All in the same day. In case that wasn't clear.

Crappy Husband would like this to happen occasionally:

Every day. In case that wasn't clear.

For variety, he'll also settle for sex and a pizza. And I'll settle for candles and flowers.

Marriage is about compromise.

FOREPLAY THEN VERSUS NOW

When we were dating (and married without kids), this was his preferred method of foreplay:

He'd enter a room and loudly announce the existence of his penis.

This worked enough times that he still does it.
But now, two kids later:

It isn't nearly as effective.

For me, when we were dating (and married without kids), this was my preferred method of foreplay:

A glass of wine and a massage worked like magic to put me in the mood.

Now, two kids later, this same combination still works like magic.

Works like magic to put me to sleep.

THE QUICKIE WINDOW

Quickies happen when you are married and have busy lives.

They are the microwaved food of the marital sex world. Convenient. Fast. Not particularly great . . . but just satisfying enough that you'll do it again soon.

Married with kids quickies are a totally different brand than the ones you enjoyed back in the early steamy days of your pre-kid life.

Back then, quickies involved clothes being ripped off with each other's teeth and dishes being thrown off the table. Delicious.

Quickies are different now.

Parents don't even take their clothes off for quickies. There's no time for that romantic shit. We just make the necessary parts accessible and then plug in.

Hurry up, the kids are banging at the door!

But sometimes even quickies are hard to come by when you have little kids.

That's like admitting, "I'm starving, but I can't use the microwave because the kids are standing right in front of it."

Kids are the world's best cock blockers. And it makes sense evolutionarily. Sex leads to babies and babies should be avoided. Another sibling just means someone else will have a stake in the popsicles in the freezer. Sex = babies = fewer popsicles.

So you have to find the right window of opportunity for your quickies. Distraction methods like TV work well. Did you know that TV programming for children was invented so parents could still have sex during daylight hours? I mean, probably.

Crappy Husband is notoriously bad at determining whether or not there is a quickie opportunity. To him, there is always a quickie opportunity. He is way too optimistic.

Kids are looking out the window at a squirrel for two seconds? Quickie!

Kids are fighting over a toy but nobody is bleeding? Quickie!

He invents these windows. They don't actually exist.

I'm more pragmatic about identifying actual quickie windows, so sometimes we don't agree.

The other day . . .

We're all in the kitchen and I just gave the kids popsicles.

Translation: Quickie!

I laugh and say I don't really think we've stumbled on a true quickie window. Sure, they have treats that will keep them occupied for ninety seconds, but they're being rather clingy today. It isn't going to work.

He says, "No, you're wrong! It is a quickie window! Let's just sneak away. They aren't even paying attention!"

Just then Crappy Boy turns around and says:

Not paying attention, eh?

Moments later Crappy Boy leaves the room. Crappy Baby follows him.

Crappy Husband is hopeful again. The window reopened! "See? They're leaving the room. We can sneak away! This is the perfect window!"

Is he right? I'm still not sure.

We start to sneak away.

I hear the sound of a window shutting in my head.

So I point to the wall and say:

And Crappy Baby explodes with laughter.

Nope. There wasn't.

ORGASMS AND MY WILLINGNESS
TO MAKE SANDWICHES

The problem with having sex is that you have to be awake and you have to move your body a little bit. This seems like an impossible task if you are exhausted. Sleep always wins.

When I feel run-down and spread thin, any request is asking too much. If I go into the kitchen to make myself a sandwich, I can't possibly be expected to make one for anyone else. All I've done ALL DAY is do things for other people. I just want to be alone!

Doesn't he realize that I've had kids hanging on me all day? Literally? The last thing I want now is someone *inside* of me. I just want my body to myself! I don't want anyone touching me for at least ten minutes. And then I want to sleep!

However, when the effort is made, the payoff is huge. When I do have an orgasm, my entire outlook on marriage, life, the universe and everything changes.

It is so worth it! For both of us!

My scientific research has shown that wives who have orgasms make 89 percent more sandwiches for their husbands. It isn't always easy. Husbands may have to do laundry or dishes or hire a babysitter even to make it happen. But in the end you might get a sandwich.

NORMAL, HUMAN SEX

So the other night we're sitting on the couch. The kids are asleep.

Crappy Husband gives me the look. He thinks I have my period so the look is of the "Blow job?" variety. You know the one. It is the one with the eyebrows and then he looks down at his crotch.

(Yes, I know we can have sex during my period. It is totally legal. We did it all the time back when we were dating. However, my periods are significantly more messy now after having kids. Period sex involves laying down surgical chux pads to protect surfaces from pools of blood and he winds up looking like he gutted a shark with his penis. It's scary.)

I explain that my period is over already.

Laughing, we start listing animals and other random life forms.

Of course then this happens:

The only type of sex we had was none.

SEX DRIVE COMPARISON CHARTS

We have very different sex drives. His is steady and stable.

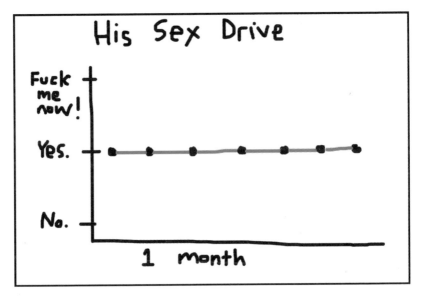

It is like driving on a flat highway in South Dakota where all you see is corn. Except switch seeing corn for wanting to have sex.

My sex drive is more like driving over a very steep mountain.

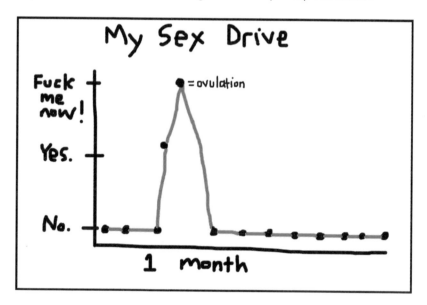

It is scary and exciting for a moment, but then you're quickly below sea level again.

THE SEX TENT

It's summer. The kids convince us to put the tent up in the backyard. They play in it during the day, but they don't want to sleep in it at night. So it just sits there. Empty.

After the kids are asleep in the house, we head out to the tent with a few blankets.

Since the kids' bedroom is right next to our bedroom and since they usually wind up sleeping in our bedroom anyway, we have to get creative with where we have sex. This is one of those creative times.

And the backyard is the perfect sex location! It's romantic! It's the perfect breezy summer temperature and we can see the stars! It's private and there is zero risk of the kids walking in on us, since we'd hear the sliding back door if they came outside. Plus, no pets are watching from the sidelines. It is absolutely perfect! Our sex life is rejuvenated.

Night after night we head out to the backyard tent. We even bring a few candles. And a bottle of lemongrass-scented massage oil. And another blanket. And a pillow. The tent is a fully stocked sex tent.

The kids show no interest in the tent after that first day. They don't even go inside it during the day. It's ours, all ours. Weeks go by and the tent stands strong.

At one point, our elderly next-door neighbor asks:

Which I think is really her way of saying, "Are you ever going to take that ugly tent down?"

But we pay no attention. Nothing is going to get in the way of our freedom and newfound sexual liberation. That tent will stay up forever.

Until one morning:

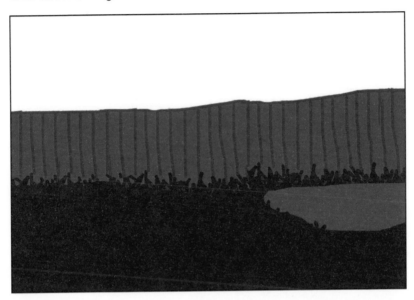

It is gone! It completely disappeared. The only thing remaining is a brown patch of dead grass. I'm shocked and confused and angry. Someone stole our sex tent? Who stole our sex tent? Why would someone steal it?

As I step outside to look for clues, the wind whips my hair and clothes.

Then I see it, across my neighbor's yard, ties flicking in the wind and all lopsided.

The heavy winds last night must have managed to fling it up over the fence. Then it tumbled across my neighbor's yard, where it snagged itself on a mulberry tree.

To make it even more embarrassing, I notice that the half-used bottle of massage oil is lying on my neighbor's grass. And a pillow. We left the tent's door unzipped! All of the sex tent contents spilled out and are now on display on her lawn!

I perform the walk of shame as I walk across my neighbor's yard and collect our things and chuck them over the fence back onto our yard.

Then I work as quickly as I can, trying to disentangle the poor, shredded tent from the tree and the surrounding bushes. It is a large tent and the poles are still in the sleeves, so I have to stand there and dismantle the entire thing. It is taking an excruciatingly long time and I'm frantic, hoping not to be seen.

But my worst fear comes true. I hear the familiar creak of my neighbor's door swinging open. She casually walks over to me and says something about the heavy winds last night. I'm mortified and apologize profusely about keeping the tent up for so long.

To my complete shock, she tells me not to worry about it at all.
Then, with a knowing wink:

She has never been so right.

CHAPTER 9

ANXIETY
OR HUSBAND)

All of the following stories happened while under the influence of female hormones.

This is the part of the book where you'll want to send Crappy Husband a bottle of vodka or a batch of cookies out of pity.

I'm not always like this. Just every month.

PMS DETECTION

Everything is going wrong. I'm a mess. My sky is falling. I have no idea why. What is happening? Why is everything so horrible?

My life is ruined.

He reminds me that I had a midlife crisis last month too.

And the month before that.

Women vary in terms of how they respond to the mention of PMS. Some get angry and throw things. Some cry. Some implode. Some morph into fire-breathing dragons and eat people.

But I've always reacted with complete relief. I actually thank him if he reminds me. Huge sigh of relief. I'm not going insane! My life isn't actually ruined! I'll be totally fine!

Until next month when I forget and it happens all over again.

JUST DON'T TALK TO ME

There is one time when nobody should ever talk to me. Never, ever. When I'm getting ready.

Not just ready for a normal day, but getting ready for something special. A dinner or a party or some other fancy function.

I'm just not myself. I'm an angry, self-conscious version of myself, a rabid hyena. Not particularly pleasant to share a confined space with.

I'll stand in front of my closet and try things on and then take them off and then try things on and then take those off and then put the original thing back on, but with a variation. It is a very complicated process of elimination that always results in me selecting the same exact outfit I wear to every fancy function.

This ritual is sacred. It is a personal form of self-flagellation that I must endure.

Nobody can intervene or they are putting themselves in great danger. Crappy Husband has learned this over the years, but sometimes he forgets and he does something stupid. He speaks to me.

He sees me wearing what he presumes is my chosen outfit and gives me a compliment. How dare he!

I'm many outfits away from being ready.

Realizing this, he asks for a time estimate. Which, really, is the worst possible thing to say. I am so absorbed in my angry ritual that time does not exist. But he reminds me and now the clock is ticking and there is pressure and panic.

At this point I say that I'm not going. Which is his cue to leave the room.

He adds that he loves me, but even that makes me angry.

Thankfully, we don't go to fancy functions very often. And I've learned to lock the bedroom door to keep everyone safe.

DR. INTERNET SEARCH

My knee has been hurting this week so I decide to look it up on the internet. That is the answer to everything. Look it up.

The internet comes in handy for looking up really important things like movie stars' names you can't remember and what your pirate name would be, based on the color of your underwear. It also comes in handy for looking up medical questions.

The internet always has a diagnosis. And it is rarely good news.

I've diagnosed myself with so many rare diseases thanks to internet searches. I've never actually *had* any of them but I'm still thankful for the consultations. How did people take care of themselves before the internet? Did they have to go to real doctors and stuff? Imagine!

MISINTERPRETATIONS & MIND READING
Sometimes, we have misinterpretations in our lines of communication. It can go both ways.

He calls me on the phone on his way home from work and asks if I've planned anything for dinner. Which I haven't.

Since there is no dinner planned, he suggests:

Rather than be grateful, which would be the sane response, it makes me furious.

For some reason, in my mind, what he is really saying is that I'm a huge failure. Clearly, what he really wants is a 1950s housewife with dinner waiting for him on the table who doesn't have her own career or interests and only lives to clean the house until she dies of boredom. (I'd also wear heels and dresses and aprons, so that part isn't so bad, I guess.)

He really just wants to pick up some burritos and come home.

Misinterpretations usually happen when I attach hidden meanings to his words. But they aren't actually there. He is a dude. He says what he means. It is simple. When I remember this, things are much easier.

I, on the other hand, am not a dude. I'm a woman. I often attach hidden meanings to *my* words. They are like little directional signs to help him. I don't always take the easy route and say what I mean. Instead, I say something else entirely with added directional signs tossed in that will help Crappy Husband arrive at the right conclusion.

The other week he asked if I wanted to go to a late movie. It was a movie that I didn't particularly want to see. Also, it was late and I had to be up early the next morning.

But this was my answer:

He didn't see any of my three directional signs! You can see them, right? Arms crossed, which is saying, "No, please protect my body from this movie." The subtle way I stated, "Well, we could go . . ." was really me saying that *in theory* we *could* go. Not that we actually *should* go. Then I followed it up with a question about the lateness, which was clearly me stating that it was much too late.

Then I got annoyed when he bought movie tickets online, since I didn't even want to go.

We replay our conversation and I explain that he completely misinterpreted my movie interest.

He may call it mind reading, but I call it navigating a conversation.

P.S. We went to the late movie and it was great. Oops. Sorry, dear. You were right. Again.

ANXIETY

There have been a few times when I've experienced above-average bouts of anxiety. Like when I have to fly on an airplane. Or speak in front of an audience. Or sometimes for reasons I can't explain.

The kids are about to take a horseback-riding class in the mountains. They've taken the class before so there is no logical reason for me to be terrified about it. But I am. It's the night before and I'm in a panic over it.

Crappy Husband asks me what I'm so worried about.

I expect him to try to tell me things that will attempt to fix the problem. To talk about reality and probability and stuff like that.

Instead, he pauses for a moment and then simply says:

THE DREAM

One morning I wake up from a horrible dream. I dreamt that Crappy Husband met a woman with a bun in her hair on a train. They talked about Mozart. He instantly fell in love with her and they moved to Spain.

I tell him the dream and we laugh about it. However, the weird part is that I'm angry with him. The real-life him. I can't shake the feeling, but I know it is ridiculous. So I try to hide it.

At one point, he catches me scowling at him.

So I admit that I'm still caught up in the feelings of the dream.

He reads my mind. You see, I've had my share of strangely prophetic dreams. But it can be hard to know when one is or isn't.

And I did. Eventually. (It has been twelve years since I had this dream. I still feel annoyed when I think about it. Or when I listen to Mozart.)

CRAPPY DOG'S MOODS

We have a little dog that we rescued last year. He is part pug and part something else and he has unfortunately (for him) decided to attach himself to me.

I have no idea how he came to the conclusion that taking his cues from me would be a good idea. Crappy Husband would have been a much better choice.

Crappy Dog is a mirror of my moods. When I'm feeling tired and lethargic, he is my loyal couch potato. When I'm feeling happy and energetic, he runs around the house and slides into walls.

Unfortunately, this means he gets PMS. All month he is happy and content.

Until:

When he has PMS he growls at the cats if they get too close to him. He tires easily and craves baked goods. He doesn't want to go on walks, he just wants to lie on the couch with a blanket and watch British comedies on Netflix.

If Crappy Husband ever wants to know how I'm feeling, he just has to look at Crappy Dog and act accordingly.

I've found that chocolate also helps him a great deal when I eat it. Because really, chocolate helps everyone.

PERFECT

When I was writing this book, I often asked Crappy Husband for ideas to keep a balance of our perspectives. Of course it isn't balanced since I wrote it, but at least the thought was there.

And this is why *he* is perfect.